Welcome Baby

Stick your favorite picture here

Guest

My Predictions

Baby's date of birth

Time of birth

Hours of labor

Baby weight

Baby height

Hair color

Eye color

Name suggestion

First word

Advice for Parents

Wishes for Baby

Guest

My Predictions

Baby's date of birth

Time of birth

Hours of labor

Baby weight

Baby height

Hair color

Eye color

Name suggestion

First word

Advice for Parents

Wishes for Baby

Guest

My Predictions

Baby's date of birth

Time of birth

Hours of labor

Baby weight

Baby height

Hair color

Eye color

Name suggestion

First word

Advice for Parents

Wishes for Baby

Guest

My Predictions

Baby's date of birth

Time of birth

Hours of labor

Baby weight

Baby height

Hair color

Eye color

Name suggestion

First word

Advice for Parents

_____

_____

Wishes for Baby

_____

_____

Guest

My Predictions

Baby's date of birth

Time of birth

Hours of labor

Baby weight

Baby height

Hair color

Eye color

Name suggestion

First word

Advice for Parents

_____

_____

Wishes for Baby

_____

_____

Guest

My Predictions

Baby's date of birth	Time of birth	Hours of labor

Baby weight	Baby height

Hair color	Eye color

Name suggestion	First word

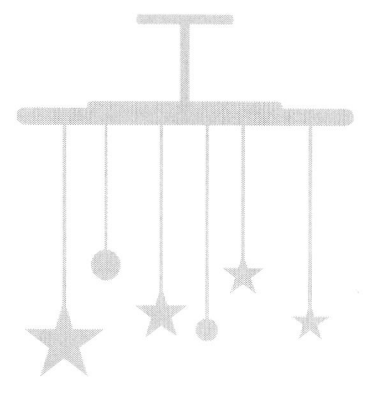

Advice for Parents

Wishes for Baby

Guest

_____

My Predictions

Baby's date of birth

Time of birth

Hours of labor

Baby weight

Baby height

Hair color

Eye color

Name suggestion

First word

Advice for Parents

_____
_____

Wishes for Baby

_____
_____

Guest

My Predictions

Baby's date of birth	Time of birth	Hours of labor

Baby weight	Baby height

Hair color	Eye color

Name suggestion	First word

Advice for Parents

Wishes for Baby

Guest

My Predictions

Baby's date of birth Time of birth Hours of labor

Baby weight Baby height

Hair color Eye color

Name suggestion First word

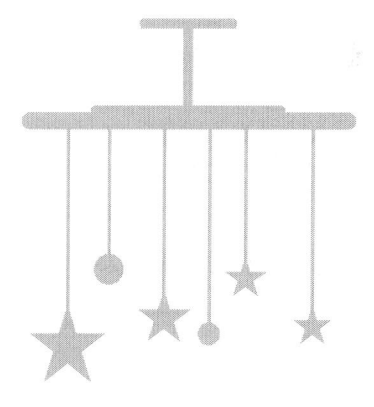

Advice for Parents

Wishes for Baby

Guest

My Predictions

Baby's date of birth   Time of birth   Hours of labor

Baby weight   Baby height

Hair color   Eye color

Name suggestion   First word

Advice for Parents

Wishes for Baby

Guest

My Predictions

Baby's date of birth

Time of birth

Hours of labor

Baby weight

Baby height

Hair color

Eye color

Name suggestion

First word

Advice for Parents

_____

_____

Wishes for Baby

_____

_____

Guest

My Predictions

Baby's date of birth   Time of birth   Hours of labor

Baby weight   Baby height

Hair color   Eye color

Name suggestion   First word

Advice for Parents

Wishes for Baby

Guest

My Predictions

Baby's date of birth

Time of birth

Hours of labor

Baby weight

Baby height

Hair color

Eye color

Name suggestion

First word

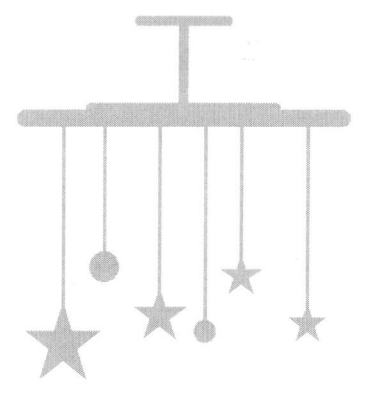

Advice for Parents

Wishes for Baby

Guest

My Predictions

Baby's date of birth	Time of birth	Hours of labor

Baby weight	Baby height

Hair color	Eye color

Name suggestion	First word

Advice for Parents

Wishes for Baby

Guest

_____

My Predictions

Baby's date of birth

Time of birth

Hours of labor

Baby weight

Baby height

Hair color

Eye color

Name suggestion

First word

Advice for Parents

_____

_____

Wishes for Baby

_____

_____

Guest

My Predictions

Baby's date of birth

Time of birth

Hours of labor

Baby weight

Baby height

Hair color

Eye color

Name suggestion

First word

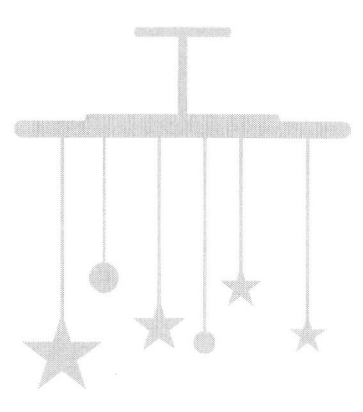

Advice for Parents

Wishes for Baby

Guest

_____

My Predictions

Baby's date of birth   Time of birth   Hours of labor

Baby weight   Baby height

Hair color   Eye color

Name suggestion   First word

Advice for Parents

_____
_____

Wishes for Baby

_____
_____

Guest

_____

My Predictions

Baby's date of birth   Time of birth   Hours of labor

Baby weight   Baby height

Hair color   Eye color

Name suggestion   First word

Advice for Parents

_____
_____

Wishes for Baby

_____
_____

Guest

My Predictions

Baby's date of birth

Time of birth

Hours of labor

Baby weight

Baby height

Hair color

Eye color

Name suggestion

First word

Advice for Parents

_____

_____

Wishes for Baby

_____

_____

Guest

My Predictions

Baby's date of birth   Time of birth   Hours of labor

Baby weight   Baby height

Hair color   Eye color

Name suggestion   First word

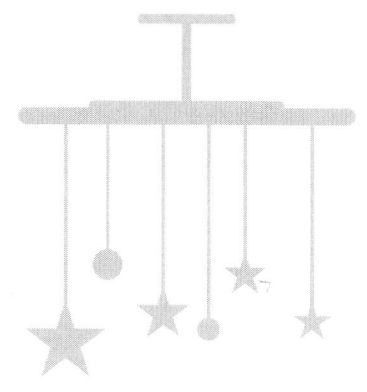

Advice for Parents

_____
_____

Wishes for Baby

_____
_____

Guest

_____

My Predictions

Baby's date of birth

Time of birth

Hours of labor

Baby weight

Baby height

Hair color

Eye color

Name suggestion

First word

Advice for Parents

_____
_____

Wishes for Baby

_____
_____

Guest

My Predictions

Baby's date of birth

Time of birth

Hours of labor

Baby weight

Baby height

Hair color

Eye color

Name suggestion

First word

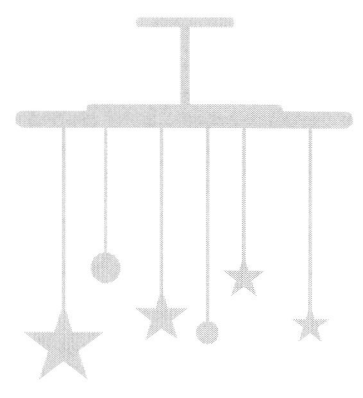

Advice for Parents

Wishes for Baby

Guest

My Predictions

Baby's date of birth

Time of birth

Hours of labor

Baby weight

Baby height

Hair color

Eye color

Name suggestion

First word

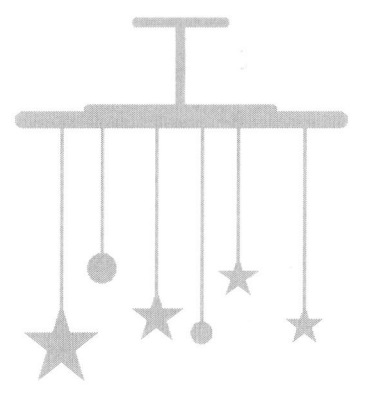

Advice for Parents

Wishes for Baby

Guest

My Predictions

Baby's date of birth

Time of birth

Hours of labor

Baby weight

Baby height

Hair color

Eye color

Name suggestion

First word

Advice for Parents

_____

_____

Wishes for Baby

_____

_____

Guest

My Predictions

Baby's date of birth

Time of birth

Hours of labor

Baby weight

Baby height

Hair color

Eye color

Name suggestion

First word

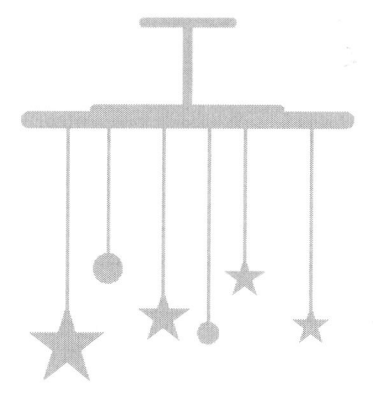

Advice for Parents

Wishes for Baby

Guest

My Predictions

Baby's date of birth

Time of birth

Hours of labor

Baby weight

Baby height

Hair color

Eye color

Name suggestion

First word

Advice for Parents

Wishes for Baby

Guest

My Predictions

Baby's date of birth　　　Time of birth　　　Hours of labor

Baby weight　　　Baby height

Hair color　　　Eye color

Name suggestion　　　First word

Advice for Parents

Wishes for Baby

Guest

My Predictions

Baby's date of birth

Time of birth

Hours of labor

Baby weight

Baby height

Hair color

Eye color

Name suggestion

First word

Advice for Parents

Wishes for Baby

Guest

_____

My Predictions

Baby's date of birth   Time of birth   Hours of labor

Baby weight   Baby height

Hair color   Eye color

Name suggestion   First word

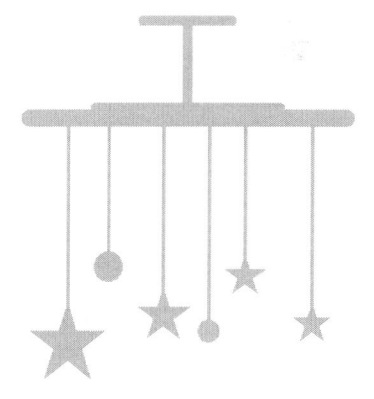

Advice for Parents

_____
_____

Wishes for Baby

_____
_____

Guest

My Predictions

Baby's date of birth　　　　Time of birth　　　　Hours of labor

Baby weight　　　　Baby height

Hair color　　　　Eye color

Name suggestion　　　　First word

Advice for Parents

Wishes for Baby

Guest

_____

My Predictions

Baby's date of birth

Time of birth

Hours of labor

Baby weight

Baby height

Hair color

Eye color

Name suggestion

First word

Advice for Parents

_____
_____

Wishes for Baby

_____
_____

Guest

My Predictions

Baby's date of birth

Time of birth

Hours of labor

Baby weight

Baby height

Hair color

Eye color

Name suggestion

First word

Advice for Parents

Wishes for Baby

Guest

_____

My Predictions

Baby's date of birth

Time of birth

Hours of labor

Baby weight

Baby height

Hair color

Eye color

Name suggestion

First word

Advice for Parents

_____
_____

Wishes for Baby

_____
_____

Guest

My Predictions

Baby's date of birth

Time of birth

Hours of labor

Baby weight

Baby height

Hair color

Eye color

Name suggestion

First word

Advice for Parents

_____

_____

Wishes for Baby

_____

_____

Guest

_____

My Predictions

Baby's date of birth

Time of birth

Hours of labor

Baby weight

Baby height

Hair color

Eye color

Name suggestion

First word

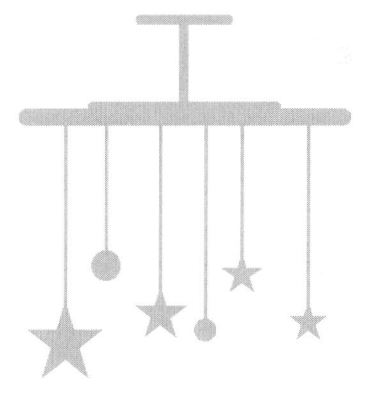

Advice for Parents

_____
_____

Wishes for Baby

_____
_____

Guest

My Predictions

Baby's date of birth

Time of birth

Hours of labor

Baby weight

Baby height

Hair color

Eye color

Name suggestion

First word

Advice for Parents

_____

_____

Wishes for Baby

_____

_____

Guest

My Predictions

Baby's date of birth

Time of birth

Hours of labor

Baby weight

Baby height

Hair color

Eye color

Name suggestion

First word

Advice for Parents

_____

_____

Wishes for Baby

_____

_____

Guest

My Predictions

Baby's date of birth

Time of birth

Hours of labor

Baby weight

Baby height

Hair color

Eye color

Name suggestion

First word

Advice for Parents

Wishes for Baby

Guest

My Predictions

Baby's date of birth

Time of birth

Hours of labor

Baby weight

Baby height

Hair color

Eye color

Name suggestion

First word

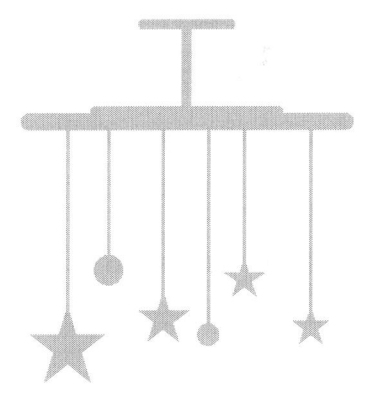

Advice for Parents

Wishes for Baby

Guest

My Predictions

Baby's date of birth

Time of birth

Hours of labor

Baby weight

Baby height

Hair color

Eye color

Name suggestion

First word

Advice for Parents

_____

_____

Wishes for Baby

_____

_____

Guest

_____

My Predictions

Baby's date of birth

Time of birth

Hours of labor

Baby weight

Baby height

Hair color

Eye color

Name suggestion

First word

Advice for Parents

_____
_____

Wishes for Baby

_____
_____

Guest

My Predictions

Baby's date of birth

Time of birth

Hours of labor

Baby weight

Baby height

Hair color

Eye color

Name suggestion

First word

Advice for Parents

Wishes for Baby

Guest

_____

My Predictions

Baby's date of birth   Time of birth   Hours of labor

Baby weight   Baby height

Hair color   Eye color

Name suggestion   First word

Advice for Parents

_____
_____

Wishes for Baby

_____
_____

Guest

My Predictions

Baby's date of birth   Time of birth   Hours of labor

Baby weight   Baby height

Hair color   Eye color

Name suggestion   First word

Advice for Parents

Wishes for Baby

Guest

My Predictions

Baby's date of birth

Time of birth

Hours of labor

Baby weight

Baby height

Hair color

Eye color

Name suggestion

First word

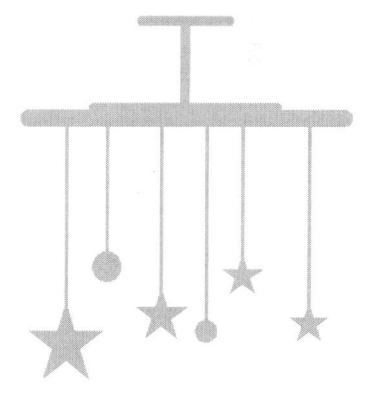

Advice for Parents

Wishes for Baby

Guest

My Predictions

Baby's date of birth

Time of birth

Hours of labor

Baby weight

Baby height

Hair color

Eye color

Name suggestion

First word

Advice for Parents

Wishes for Baby

Guest

My Predictions

Baby's date of birth

Time of birth

Hours of labor

Baby weight

Baby height

Hair color

Eye color

Name suggestion

First word

Advice for Parents

Wishes for Baby

Guest

My Predictions

Baby's date of birth

Time of birth

Hours of labor

Baby weight

Baby height

Hair color

Eye color

Name suggestion

First word

Advice for Parents

_____

_____

Wishes for Baby

_____

_____

Guest

My Predictions

Baby's date of birth

Time of birth

Hours of labor

Baby weight

Baby height

Hair color

Eye color

Name suggestion

First word

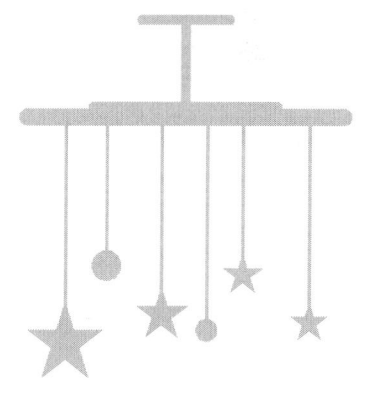

Advice for Parents

_____

_____

Wishes for Baby

_____

_____

Guest

_____

My Predictions

Baby's date of birth		Time of birth		Hours of labor

Baby weight		Baby height

Hair color		Eye color

Name suggestion		First word

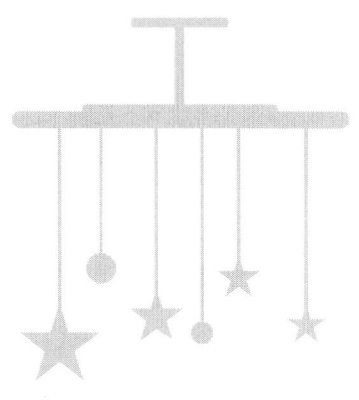

Advice for Parents

_____
_____

Wishes for Baby

_____
_____

Guest

My Predictions

Baby's date of birth

Time of birth

Hours of labor

Baby weight

Baby height

Hair color

Eye color

Name suggestion

First word

Advice for Parents

Wishes for Baby

Guest

My Predictions

Baby's date of birth

Time of birth

Hours of labor

Baby weight

Baby height

Hair color

Eye color

Name suggestion

First word

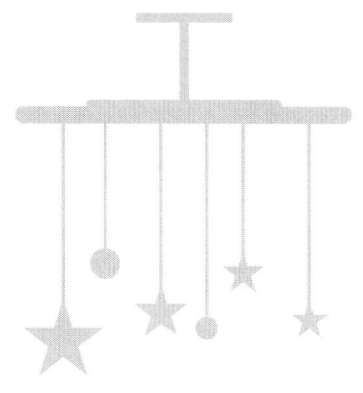

Advice for Parents

_____

_____

Wishes for Baby

_____

_____

Guest

My Predictions

Baby's date of birth

Time of birth

Hours of labor

Baby weight

Baby height

Hair color

Eye color

Name suggestion

First word

Advice for Parents

Wishes for Baby

Guest

My Predictions

Baby's date of birth

Time of birth

Hours of labor

Baby weight

Baby height

Hair color

Eye color

Name suggestion

First word

Advice for Parents

Wishes for Baby

Guest

My Predictions

Baby's date of birth

Time of birth

Hours of labor

Baby weight

Baby height

Hair color

Eye color

Name suggestion

First word

Advice for Parents

Wishes for Baby

Guest

My Predictions

Baby's date of birth

Time of birth

Hours of labor

Baby weight

Baby height

Hair color

Eye color

Name suggestion

First word

Advice for Parents

_____

_____

Wishes for Baby

_____

_____

Guest

My Predictions

Baby's date of birth

Time of birth

Hours of labor

Baby weight

Baby height

Hair color

Eye color

Name suggestion

First word

Advice for Parents

Wishes for Baby

Guest

_____

My Predictions

Baby's date of birth   Time of birth   Hours of labor

Baby weight   Baby height

Hair color   Eye color

Name suggestion   First word

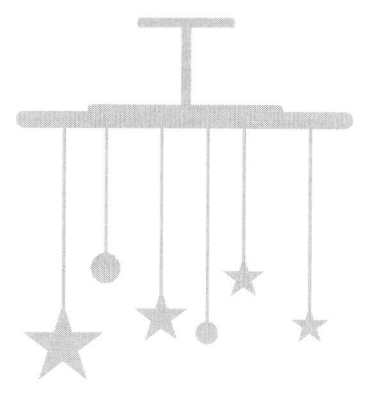

Advice for Parents

_____
_____

Wishes for Baby

_____
_____

Guest

My Predictions

Baby's date of birth

Time of birth

Hours of labor

Baby weight

Baby height

Hair color

Eye color

Name suggestion

First word

Advice for Parents

Wishes for Baby

Guest

My Predictions

Baby's date of birth

Time of birth

Hours of labor

Baby weight

Baby height

Hair color

Eye color

Name suggestion

First word

Advice for Parents

_____

_____

Wishes for Baby

_____

_____

Guest

My Predictions

Baby's date of birth   Time of birth   Hours of labor

Baby weight   Baby height

Hair color   Eye color

Name suggestion   First word

Advice for Parents

_____
_____

Wishes for Baby

_____
_____

Guest

My Predictions

Baby's date of birth

Time of birth

Hours of labor

Baby weight

Baby height

Hair color

Eye color

Name suggestion

First word

Advice for Parents

Wishes for Baby

Guest

My Predictions

Baby's date of birth

Time of birth

Hours of labor

Baby weight

Baby height

Hair color

Eye color

Name suggestion

First word

Advice for Parents

Wishes for Baby

Guest

My Predictions

Baby's date of birth

Time of birth

Hours of labor

Baby weight

Baby height

Hair color

Eye color

Name suggestion

First word

Advice for Parents

Wishes for Baby

Guest

My Predictions

Baby's date of birth

Time of birth

Hours of labor

Baby weight

Baby height

Hair color

Eye color

Name suggestion

First word

Advice for Parents

Wishes for Baby

Guest

My Predictions

Baby's date of birth

Time of birth

Hours of labor

Baby weight

Baby height

Hair color

Eye color

Name suggestion

First word

Advice for Parents

Wishes for Baby

Guest

My Predictions

Baby's date of birth

Time of birth

Hours of labor

Baby weight

Baby height

Hair color

Eye color

Name suggestion

First word

Advice for Parents

Wishes for Baby

Guest

My Predictions

Baby's date of birth						Time of birth						Hours of labor

Baby weight						Baby height

Hair color						Eye color

Name suggestion						First word

Advice for Parents

_____

_____

Wishes for Baby

_____

_____

Guest

My Predictions

Baby's date of birth　　　　Time of birth　　　　Hours of labor

Baby weight　　　　　　　　Baby height

Hair color　　　　　　　　　Eye color

Name suggestion　　　　　　First word

Advice for Parents

Wishes for Baby

Guest

_____

My Predictions

Baby's date of birth   Time of birth   Hours of labor

Baby weight   Baby height

Hair color   Eye color

Name suggestion   First word

Advice for Parents

_____
_____

Wishes for Baby

_____
_____

Guest

My Predictions

Baby's date of birth

Time of birth

Hours of labor

Baby weight

Baby height

Hair color

Eye color

Name suggestion

First word

Advice for Parents

_____
_____

Wishes for Baby

_____
_____

Guest

_____

My Predictions

Baby's date of birth   Time of birth   Hours of labor

Baby weight   Baby height

Hair color   Eye color

Name suggestion   First word

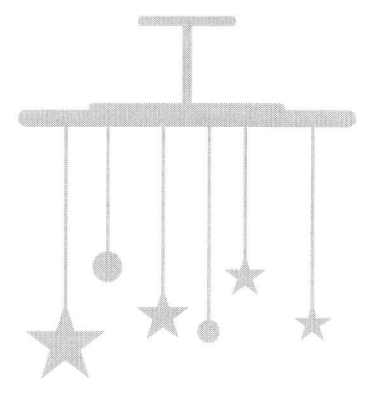

Advice for Parents

_____
_____

Wishes for Baby

_____
_____

Guest

My Predictions

Baby's date of birth

Time of birth

Hours of labor

Baby weight

Baby height

Hair color

Eye color

Name suggestion

First word

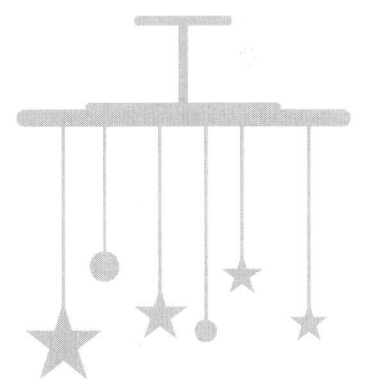

Advice for Parents

Wishes for Baby

Guest

_____

My Predictions

Baby's date of birth	Time of birth	Hours of labor

Baby weight	Baby height

Hair color	Eye color

Name suggestion	First word

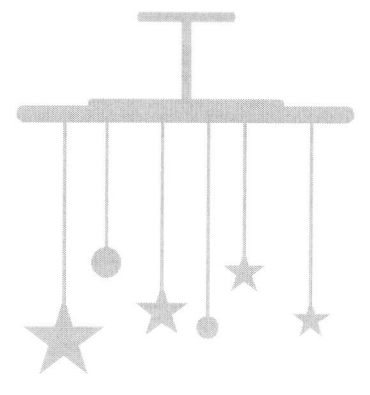

Advice for Parents

_____
_____

Wishes for Baby

_____
_____

Guest

My Predictions

Baby's date of birth

Time of birth

Hours of labor

Baby weight

Baby height

Hair color

Eye color

Name suggestion

First word

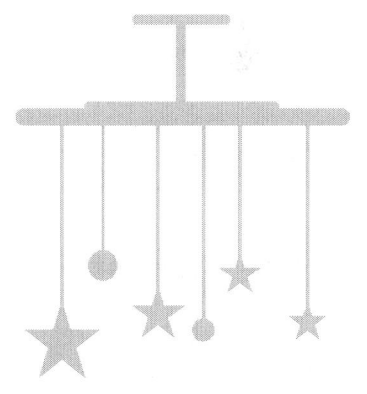

Advice for Parents

Wishes for Baby

Guest

My Predictions

Baby's date of birth   Time of birth   Hours of labor

Baby weight   Baby height

Hair color   Eye color

Name suggestion   First word

Advice for Parents

_____
_____

Wishes for Baby

_____
_____

Guest

_____

My Predictions

Baby's date of birth   Time of birth   Hours of labor

Baby weight   Baby height

Hair color   Eye color

Name suggestion   First word

Advice for Parents

_____
_____

Wishes for Baby

_____
_____

Guest

My Predictions

Baby's date of birth   Time of birth   Hours of labor

Baby weight   Baby height

Hair color   Eye color

Name suggestion   First word

Advice for Parents

Wishes for Baby

Guest

My Predictions

Baby's date of birth

Time of birth

Hours of labor

Baby weight

Baby height

Hair color

Eye color

Name suggestion

First word

Advice for Parents

Wishes for Baby

Guest

My Predictions

Baby's date of birth	Time of birth	Hours of labor

Baby weight	Baby height

Hair color	Eye color

Name suggestion	First word

Advice for Parents

Wishes for Baby

Guest

My Predictions

Baby's date of birth

Time of birth

Hours of labor

Baby weight

Baby height

Hair color

Eye color

Name suggestion

First word

Advice for Parents

Wishes for Baby

Guest

My Predictions

Baby's date of birth

Time of birth

Hours of labor

Baby weight

Baby height

Hair color

Eye color

Name suggestion

First word

Advice for Parents

Wishes for Baby

Guest

My Predictions

Baby's date of birth

Time of birth

Hours of labor

Baby weight

Baby height

Hair color

Eye color

Name suggestion

First word

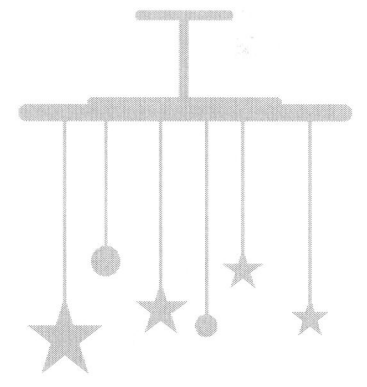

Advice for Parents

Wishes for Baby

Guest

My Predictions

Baby's date of birth   Time of birth   Hours of labor

Baby weight   Baby height

Hair color   Eye color

Name suggestion   First word

Advice for Parents

Wishes for Baby

Guest

My Predictions

Baby's date of birth

Time of birth

Hours of labor

Baby weight

Baby height

Hair color

Eye color

Name suggestion

First word

Advice for Parents

Wishes for Baby

Guest

My Predictions

Baby's date of birth

Time of birth

Hours of labor

Baby weight

Baby height

Hair color

Eye color

Name suggestion

First word

Advice for Parents

Wishes for Baby

Guest

My Predictions

Baby's date of birth

Time of birth

Hours of labor

Baby weight

Baby height

Hair color

Eye color

Name suggestion

First word

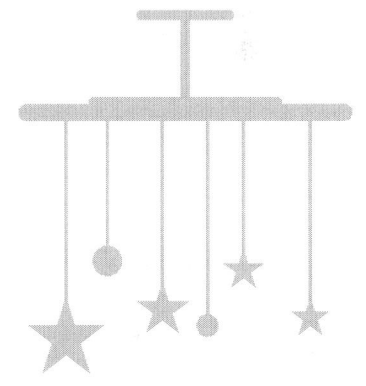

Advice for Parents

Wishes for Baby

Guest

My Predictions

Baby's date of birth

Time of birth

Hours of labor

Baby weight

Baby height

Hair color

Eye color

Name suggestion

First word

Advice for Parents

_____

_____

Wishes for Baby

_____

_____

Guest

My Predictions

Baby's date of birth

Time of birth

Hours of labor

Baby weight

Baby height

Hair color

Eye color

Name suggestion

First word

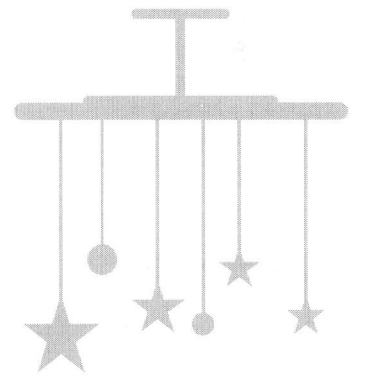

Advice for Parents

Wishes for Baby

Guest

My Predictions

Baby's date of birth

Time of birth

Hours of labor

Baby weight

Baby height

Hair color

Eye color

Name suggestion

First word

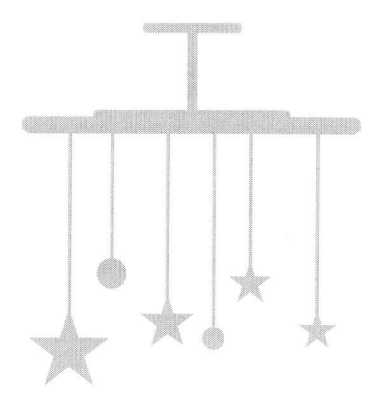

Advice for Parents

_____

_____

Wishes for Baby

_____

_____

Guest

_____

My Predictions

Baby's date of birth

Time of birth

Hours of labor

Baby weight

Baby height

Hair color

Eye color

Name suggestion

First word

Advice for Parents

_____
_____

Wishes for Baby

_____
_____

Gift Log

Gifts

Gift	Given By	Thank you note sent

Gifts

Gift	Given By	Thank you note sent

Gifts

Gift	Given By	Thank you note sent

Gifts

Gift	Given By	Thank you note sent

Gifts

Gift	Given By	Thank you note sent

Gifts

Gift	Given By	Thank you note sent

Gifts

Gift	Given By	Thank you note sent

Gifts

Gift	Given By	Thank you note sent

Gifts

Gift	Given By	Thank you note sent

Gifts

Gift	Given By	Thank you note sent

Made in the USA
Monee, IL
11 July 2023

38979382R00059